T0158226

Angelic
Wisdom

Anne Russell

authorHOUSE®

AuthorHouse™ UK
1663 Liberty Drive
Bloomington, IN 47403 USA
www.authorhouse.co.uk
Phone: 0800.197.4150

Published by AuthorHouse 09/02/2016

ISBN: 978-1-5246-6319-3 (sc)
ISBN: 978-1-5246-6318-6 (e)

CONTENTS

Epigraph

"Love is a gift that comes from within. It lights the world and creates joy unfurled as it washes away pain; tears; fears; and leaves only joy; peace; happiness and hope for tomorrow".....

Prologue

"As human beings our greatest fight is not with others, but with ourselves. Learning to know and understand who we are is key to us knowing and learning how to love ourselves. Without this knowledge and power we will never learn how to become our own best friend. Acceptance, acknowledgement of who we are and gentle, nurturing, self improvement helps our self esteem; soothes our soul; and gives us confidence and courage in a way that nothing and no one else could ever do ………………"

Land of Paradigm

Somewhere on
The edge of time
There lies a land
Of paradigm
Where peace and truth
Form its roots
And healing hands
Create its lands
Where butterflies gold
Fly in its fold
And eternal hope
Fulfils its scope
Where food is plenty
But hunters none
There is no need
To carry gun
It is a land
Beyond the pale
Where love prevails
To all avail
And angel lore
Is at the fore
To lead the way
For peaceful sway

True Sense

In the land
Of faraway dreams
Everything is all
It has ever seemed
All that we impart
And see in our heart
Manifests here
It is so very clear
Our thoughts are as real
As anything we feel
And as our mind
Clears its sign
Our thoughts become
Our new kingdom
And create a world
So new and unfurled
And help us see
True vision of clarity
As thoughts are as real
As sense of feel
And leave us with
A wisdom new
As we regain our truth
And identity anew

Echoes

Whispers, echoes
Voices dim
I hear them always
Above the skim
Of time and space
Beyond the face
Of what we perceive
And what we believe
And still they feel
Utmost and real
Although to many
They feel surreal
So if only we
Would open our soul
The voices we hear
Could make us whole

Castle Land

In our world
Of shifting sand
We need to build
A castle land
Where permanence reigns
On impermanent plane
And time and tide
Have no place to hide
Where all is plenty
And man knows not empty
And wild horses run
In freedom and sun
Where everything flows
And everyone knows
They will never know sorrow
As they plan for tomorrow

Freedom

Freedom comes
And freedom flows
It is there for all
Dependent on the call
To truly know
How we can grow
We need to be
As one and free
To have no need
Only want of other
And to know to love all
As we would our brother
Is to keep our soul
To make it whole
And know we need
No other to be complete

Happiness

Feeling bliss
Feeling the kiss
Of sun caressed trees
As they whisper in the breeze
The sound of laughter
The sound of song
The sound of children's chatter
As they play in the throng
Breathtaking sunsets
Of crimson glory
Showing such beauty
Of our earth and its story
All the creatures
Of the earth
Scurrying to feature
Their predestined dearth
And seeing the veil
Beyond the pale
Where angels in glory
Sing their everlasting story

Time

The unrelenting
Pace of time
Means there is
No finite line
From whence we came
And whence we remain
For nothing stays
It changes always
So always remember
To make the most
Of whatever you chose
And whatever does go
For if you cease
To forget your lease
Time will pass
And you will not last
For all things will
In the fullness of time
Turn to dust
And spirit sublime
So value all
Before the last fall
Open your eyes
To all that is life
Make sure you do
All that is due
And that your contract is driven
From all that is riven

Forgiveness

It is hard at times
To forget darker rhimes
And to learn to trust
As we surely must
Through earth's many planes
Until wisdom we gain
We need to remember
That learning is pain
But learning too
Is a gift so true
And as we live
We need to forgive
For all those whom
We believe have betrayed
Have hurt or dismayed
In the midst of life's haze
For maybe they
Too feel the pain
And their learning now
Will have greater gain
As they realise how
They renaged on their vow
And will seek advice

For the rest of their life
So to learn to let go
And go with life's flow
Is all that we need
If we want to pay heed
To living in love
As sent from above
For the choice is true
To live life anew

The Storm

Impending storm
The signal drawn
Birds do call
In frequent thrall
The morning hue
Is pink and blue
But beneath its veneer
The cracks do appear
Whistling breeze
Gradually does tease
Then suddenly blasts
And blows all masts
Howling like a wolf
The storm does engulf
So that all that we
Can do is flee
Or sit and wait
Until it does abate

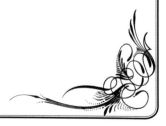

The Fight

Birds of flight
Falling light
Back to safety
Before the fight
Armour secure
Sword assured
Ready to face
The enemy's pace
Stealth is mine
As I see the sign
And then it starts
The battle imparts
Fear is gone
My mind is strong
As I fight in might
In righteous sight

Lessons

Every day I walk this way
I cherish the time I hold in my sway
All the gifts of life and love
I know are given from heaven above
All the lessons that I learn
Are here to teach me at every turn
That life is a joy and a gift so true
And helps me see the world anew

Path of Peace

Looking through the starlight glow
Makes me feel the ebb and flow
And wonder of this earth anew
To remember how my spirit flew
Long before I touched this world
Before I became as embryo unfurled
Born in to this world of man
Born to learn all that I can
Knowing that on my path of peace
Sometimes people will take their fleece
But forgiving them all as I can
Will in the end bring peace to man
As all I feel is love and joy
And though to many it may seem a ploy
I carry on through time and place
To show mankind the love on my face

Angelic Glows

They float above the trees at night
And glow translucent in our sight
Orbs of gold and silver light
Spirits borne in everlasting flight
Protecting us as we sleep in thrall
Nourishing, guarding, so we never fall
Into throes of night's dark foes
But into arms of angelic glows

Beyond the Line

What we see and what we show
Are different to the real beauty we know
On the surface of our lives
We do all we can to survive
But if only we could see beyond
Far above the material bond
There is so much to feed our soul
And our spiritual guides will make us whole
Showing the beauty that we hold
And knowing our souls can never be sold
So always remember to open your eyes
To the beauty within making you rise
Miracles happen all the time
We just need to see beyond the line
And realise what is real and true
As we view the world and its beauty anew

Earth Magic

Softly swaying in the breeze
Courtly branches of evergreen trees
Bowing down in majesty borne
Hearing the echoes of the unicorn's horn
Fairies, elves, nature's sprites
Pirouette around as they shine their lights
Beams of glory from the sun's great hold
Flow like lava of molten gold
Onto the earth's blanket of light
Giving us glorious strength of sight

Dreamland

Faraway dreams of landscapes new
Blue and gold with yellow hue
Snowscapes range in distant sight
Like flurries of clouds on a winter's night
Colours galore never before seen
Beauteous, rich colours of sheen
Stardust floats above the night
Skylines full of silver light
Dreamland fills my very soul
Healing my heart and making it whole

Love

Do I love you
Yes I do
How do I know
This love is true
Love is giving
Love is strength
Love is knowing
At any length
It never lies
It never dies
There is no due
It is always true
No matter how long
The distance does part
It will always stay strong
If you are true in your heart

Innocence

Dear baby divine
I am thine
For I am with you
All of the time
Guarding your keep
Whilst you sleep
Safe from harm
In my heavenly arm
Protecting your soul
Keeping you whole
Guarding your heart
So we never do part

Angelic Ascension

The light will come
When darkness is done
And as it raises
Its fullest praises
To our God of love
In heaven above
All around
Will hear the sound
Of ascending angels
As they abound
Singing in love
To God above
In celebration of
The dazzling sight
Of brightest light
Covering the earth
With angelic love
And angelic dearth

The Visit

I always knew
Of your grace and hue
That angelic and pure
You would help me learn more
As it is
And has always been
For all of time
It would seem
That we always
In divine timing meet
For the realm of darkness
To defeat

Angelic Protection

Only an angel
Will stand by your side
Defending you near
With you to abide
Guiding you dear
So that you can hear
Words of advice
Sent with truest device
Words of love
Sent from heaven above
Keeping you safe
Keeping the faith
Making you know
As your spirit does grow
That the true divine light
Is always in sight

Angelic Guides

At times it may seem
That no one has been
To guard you well
In all the swell
In all the maelstrom
Of your life
As you rise above
The trouble and strife
But always know
It will make you grow
And we are always near
Dear child never fear
And never will we
Let you down
Always and forever
Our love does abound

The Watchers

As we watch
Over the sway
We will return
Come what may
To bring the world
To brighter hue
To bring its fold
To such its due
Of dazzling light
So pure and bright
That human eyes
Will be more wise
And god's creation
Of every nation
Will once and for all
Hold heaven's pure thrall

New Dawn

As the new year does dawn
A new world is born
From angelics on high
Falling down from the sky
And mankind will see
That the old must flee
And in its place
The sword and the mace
Must once again be
Now as was then
To cleanse the world
And let it unfurl.
Into spiritual unity
With no trace of impunity
So that humanity can relearn
The wisdom of its ways
So that never again
Will it be lost in a haze
Of self absorbing purpose
And such destructive murkiness
And the kingdom of heaven
Will reign thus forth
Supreme, sublime and seeing
Over every earthly being

New World

And as the final curtain falls
The darkness will be void
And light will be all
Mankind will be hit
By flood and storm
And whence it has come
There will be darkness before dawn
But when the sunrise finally comes
Angelics all around will shine as suns
Bringing with them hope and light
Helping us build the world so right

The Plan

Every single living being
Is part of God's plan
All knowing all seeing
So if we deign
To serve his reign
We know as such
Our soul will touch
Shards of wondrous
Glorious light
And angels singing
In holy sight
And millions of stars
Shining en masse
To give our hearts
Such a wondrous blast
Of joy everlasting
Through eternity casting
The magic of love
From heaven above

Spiritual Warrior

Softly, softly
Tread your path
Child of God
We are so glad
That you have chosen
To come home
To that which you always
Through eternity have known
You never ever
Left our fold
You have just relearned
As was foretold
All the ancient
Wisdoms true
And for that you are
As spirit renew

Humanity

As insects are we
With our heads to the ground
So we miss the beauty
That is all around
The joy of the sunset
In its blaze of golden glory
The sound of the skylark
As it sings of dawn's own story
The constant flurries
Of cumulus clouds
The frenzy and flurries
Of the animal kingdom's crowds
The luminescent pure rays
Of the moon's translucent haze
As she guards whilst we sleep
And awakens us before her leap
Into her eternal light
Even when not in sight

True Faith

Faith is like
The first fall of snow
It is something so pure
And something you know
At times it seems
As if its sheens
Are hidden in folds
As you ignore its goals
Yet you never do
And never have
You have always been true
And for that be glad
For truly living
In the sight of God
Is far more true
Than if you do plod
On this earthplane
Drawn in to the game
And as it now is
You are touched by the kiss
Of heavenly hosts
Guarding you most
Safe from all harm
In their heavenly arm

Wings of Love

God bless the angelic
Birds of the sky
As angels do
So they do fly
To the tips
Of a universe bright
Broadening their scope
As they float in flight
Bringing a sense
Of freedom true
As they fly aloft
To see the world anew
And so for us
Our spirit can soar
Like a nightingale sing
And a lion roar
Bringing us as they
Nearer to God
As we travel along
This beauteous, earthen sod

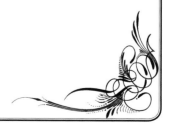

The Gift

Life is such
A gift from above
Bringing eternal light
Filled with such love
Showing how
As you take your vow
The glory of being
All knowing and seeing
Of being part
Of a universe bright
Full of heavenly beings
So pure of sight
And knowing so
You have far to go
But knowing thus far
You are part of each star
And each galaxy bright
Filled with purest light

The Game

This cat and mouse game
Is always the same
An arena where man
Does all that he can
To stay ahead
Of the human game
Lest he is caught
And comes to naught
So onward he goes
Step by step
Until all his objectives
Have been met
And then he must
In all the haze
Know who is true
And who it is that plays

Earth's Run

Always remember
As you walk this earth
To be a true friend
With integrity to the end
Who embraces all
And never judges a fall
For we are here to learn
To respect and earn
Our true self connection
And time for reflection
To show love without bound
To all those around
To work from compassion
Humility and grace
To know how to show
Love through your place
And to know as you grow
The love that you show
Will shine as the sun
Throughout your earth's run

Spirit Flow

As my spirit
Grows and flows
It floats above
As my body goes
Using its wings
It soars and sings
Using its senses
It sees no fences
All it hears
Is freedom's song
As it glides away
From the crowds and throng
Into beauteous
Star filled skies
Feeling at one
In its true kingdom

Nature's Magic

The majesty
Of all we see
Is not by chance
Is of earth's dance
Each creation
Has its station
Each design
Is our sign
Every colour
Every hue
More breathtaking
Than any view
Artist, writers
Musicians too
All try to know
This beautiful show
But in the end
There is no other blend
Than nature's true beauty
And magical duty

Intentions

That sweet, sweet scent
Of intentions well meant
Of humanity's aim
To end their game
Of strategies near
Agendas and aim
Of endless quest
For power no less
They say they wish
To raise their game
To serve the dish
Of soulful gain
As wealth and possessions
Hold no sway
But soon in truth
When they walk the path
It is not so easy
As there is much aftermath
For staying the course
Means input of much resource
And so many well meaning
See there is no longer leaning
On strength of others
As they would their brothers

And to walk the path
Of love and light
Takes more that they realised
And they need all their might
To raise their sight
And serve the light

Paradise Lost

To taste the fruit of paradise lost
Is to touch the tips at eternity's cost
For some things need to be
Elusive and forever free
And we need to know
That wherever we go
There will always be
Hidden secrets never to see
For the real truth of living
Is to never stop giving
And to realise at last
That we will never ever grasp
All the great mysteries
Of our everlasting life
For if we ever did
We would never again strive
To know the wonders of all
In our everlasting thrall

Angelic Force

As the last rays of sunlight
Leave the sky
A million angels
Float on high
To face the dearth
Of our human earth
To try to repair
The cost of mankind's lair
To fill the world
With hope and light
With star upon star
To give them sight
To shine in force
From the eternal source
To save humankind
From being so blind
To learn to think
To swim not sink
And make them whole
As man and soul

Epilogue

"And in the end it is not what you have learned that drives you forward, but that which you have yet to learn that you continue to strive for…………..
And if so you were given that infinite time to learn the wisdom of the universe, you would still only scratch the surface of time; humankind; the universe; and everything that exists beyond all horizons and all possibilities …………………"

Printed in the United States
By Bookmasters